THE CLAN DONALD

(MACDONALDS, MACDONELLS, MACALISTERS AND THEIR SEPTS)

Clansman's Badge

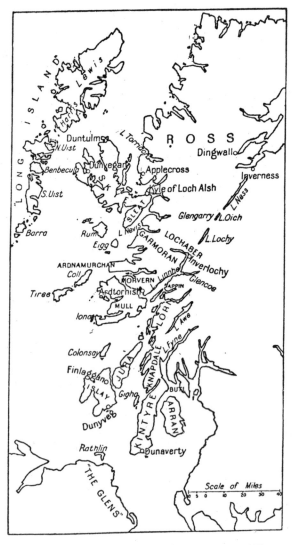

N. W. Scotland.   The territories of " The Clan Donald "

THE CLAN DONALD

(MACDONALDS, MACDONELLS, MACALISTERS AND THEIR SEPTS)

A GAELIC PRINCIPALITY AS A FOCUS OF GAELIC CULTURE

BY

I. F. GRANT, LL.D.

Author of *The Lordship of the Isles, The Social and Economic Development of Scotland before 1603*, Etc.

JOHNSTON & BACON

First published by
Johnston & Bacon 1952
New editions: 1963 and 1979

ISBN 978 07179 4521 4

© *Copyright: Famedram Publishers Ltd*
www.northernbooks.co.uk
Print: Imprint Digital Ltd

The Foundation of Clan Donald

MacDonalds may well be proud of the name they bear. Clan Donald is the largest Highland clan. It has played a part more distinguished than that of any other clan in the history of Scotland. Beyond all this, Clan Donald has a unique claim to the interest and reverence of all those who love the Gael, their language and their high traditions, and who mourn their decline, for, under the old Lords of the Isles, the chiefs of Clan Donald, a last Gaelic polity existed in Scotland. The magical beauty of the old MacDonald heritage—the Western Isles and wide stretches of the lands by the western sea—is indeed a fit setting for dreams of this vanished Gaelic principality and of what might have been, had it survived.

At the time of their greatest power, the chiefs of Clan Donald, as Lords of the Isles and Earls of Ross, with their closest followers and vassals, were firmly established in the long chain of islands from Kintyre up to the Butt of Lewis—Islay, Jura, Colonsay, Mull, Tiree, Coll, Eigg and Rum, Skye, the Uists, Lewis, with many lesser isles. They also held Kintyre, Lochaber, Ardnamurchan, the Lordship of Loch Alsh, Garmoran, Morvern, and much besides. Their hold on Central and Eastern Ross, though they enforced it again and again, was much less secure.

According to his seanachies, the Lord of the Isles was descended from Conn of the Hundred Battles, High King of Ireland, who flourished about A.D. 125, from Colla Uais, who is said to have been an Irish prince who ruled in the Islands before the establishment of the kingdom of Dalriada, and from Fergus MacErc himself, the founder of that kingdom. The pedigree is incomplete and rests only on tradition, but it was firmly believed in by the clan in the Gaelic revival that began in the Western Islands after the decline of the Norse power. They were proud to call themselves the Children of Colla, and MacMhuirich began his great Incitement to Battle, delivered before Red Harlaw, with the words :

> A Chlannaibh Chuin, cuimhnichibh
> Cruas an am na h'iorghuill.

(Sons of Conn, remember
Hardihood in time of strife.)

Also Mary MacLeod, the famous seventeenth-century poetess, described Clan Donald as " The race of Colla of vast armies and many tributes ; with their full laden, white-sailed fleet as they sail upon the ocean." [1]

With Somerled we are on historical ground. He laid the foundations on which the power of Clan Donald arose. His name is Norse, but that of his father, Gille Brìghde, is Gaelic. Gille Brìghde is said to have been driven from his lands, but Somerled conquered so large a part of the west that he was known as the Regulus of Argyll. He supported the Gaelic claimant to the Earldom of Moray, and he proved a formidable adversary to Malcolm IV, King of Scots. He married a daughter of the Norse King of Man ; and, when one of the dynastic struggles which afflicted that kingdom broke out, he was able

---

[1] J. Carmichael Watson, *Gaelic Songs of Mary Macleod*, p. 79.

to take possession, in his son's name, of Man itself and of all the Western Isles, which then belonged to it. He was leading another campaign against the King of Scots in 1164 at the head of 160 galleys when he was assassinated.

After Somerled's death the story of his descendants is very obscure. Apparently his mainland possessions were divided among his sons, of whom he had several besides those of his marriage with the Princess of Man. Man itself, and the islands north of Ardnamurchan, reverted to a re-established King of Man, but the islands south of Ardnamurchan were divided between the three sons of this marriage. Dougall received Mull with the adjacent islands, as well as Lorn. He was the founder of the MacDougalls, and his line was known as the Lords of Lorn. Reginald had Islay, Kintyre (which always counted as an island in those days), and a share of Arran. His line was known as the Lords of Islay. Angus had the rest of Arran and Bute. Angus and his sons were killed, and Reginald occupied his lands. Reginald had two sons, Donald, the Lord of Islay, who has given his name to Clan Donald, and who occupied Islay and Kintyre, and Ruairidh, who claimed the lands once owned by Angus. His descendants were known as the MacRuairidhs.

The situation was complicated by the fact that the final struggle between the King of Norway and the Scots king for supremacy in the Western Isles was going on, and the descendants of Somerled had to deal with the problem of divided and conflicting allegiances. Finally, in 1266 the Western Islands were ceded by Norway to Scotland.

The King of Scots (Alexander III) confirmed the

Lords of Lorn and Islay in their possessions. He gave
Skye and Lewis to the Earl of Ross, and Arran and
Bute to the Steward (who had some claim to them
through a marriage with the daughter and heiress of
the unfortunate Angus). He compensated the descendants of Ruairidh by the grant of Garmoran (the
region between Ardnamurchan and Glenelg) and the
Uists.

The Wars of Independence brought great changes
in the position. The Lord of Lorn had been a devoted
supporter of Balliol, and lost most of his lands. Alexander, Lord of Islay, had also actively supported
Balliol, but his younger brother, Angus Òg, had
sheltered Robert the Bruce, when he was a fugitive at
the lowest ebb of his fortunes, in his castle of Dunaverty,
and his presence with a great following at Bannockburn
was decisive. The King's speech to him there—" My
hope is constant in thee "—is the motto of MacDonald
of Clanranald. Angus Òg was granted the lands of
Alexander, his brother, Mull and other islands belong-
ing to MacDougall of Lorn, and also land in Lochaber
forfeited by the Comyns. The King made him resign
the strategically important lands of Kintyre. Kintyre
was, however, regained by the more devious policy of
Angus Òg's astute son, John, and he also received a
grant of Lewis. It may be noted that Robert the
Bruce gave rich rewards to another faithful adherent,
Campbell of Lochow, a name of ill omen for Clan
Donald !

John, son of Angus Òg, not only enlarged his possessions by considerable royal grants ; he also made two
successful marriages. The first was with Amy, the
heiress of the MacRuairidhs (descendants of Ruairidh,

brother of Donald), the second with Margaret, a daughter of King Robert II. John's possessions included all the Western Isles north of Kintyre (except Skye, which formed part of the Earldom of Ross), with Kintyre itself, Lochaber, Garmoran, and other lands. In 1354 John assumed the title of *Dominus Insularum*— Lord of the Isles. That he should himself have assumed this title marks his especial position and claims. In earlier times Somerled's descendants had often been referred to as the Kings of Islay, Lorn, etc. Of course, both in Ireland and in the Scandinavian Sagas, this term was freely used, and there were many kinglets with limited jurisdiction ; but all through their story the Lords of the Isles, *whenever they felt themselves able to do so,* assumed more than the position of an ordinary subject of the Scots Crown.

The Lordship of the Isles

The Lordship of the Isles lasted from 1354 till its forfeiture in 1493. There were four Lords of the Isles— John, Donald, Alexander, and a second John. They each in turn fell foul of the Scots Crown from time to time, and they did not hesitate to intrigue with the King of England. The most noteworthy occasion was in 1462, when the last Lord made the Treaty of Westminster with Edward IV, which provided for the conquest of Scotland and the division of the north of it between the Lord of the Isles himself and the Earl of Douglas. So powerful were the Lords of the Isles

that they could over-run and even sometimes occupy
and administer large parts of the north of Scotland.
No less than seven times they or their lieutenants
streamed across the Highlands and captured Inverness.
On the other hand, when a considerable part of the
man-power of Scotland was mobilised against them,
the Lords of the Isles were obliged to come to terms—
sometimes, as in the case of Alexander and the second
John, most ignominiously.

The Lords of the Isles were able to make an important addition to their great territories. Donald,
the second Lord, married the heiress to the Earldom
of Ross. Ross, with its rich eastern coastlands, and
the strategically convenient western lands and Island
of Skye, was a rich prize, and the Duke of Albany,
the Regent, had put up his son as another claimant.
The rights to the Earldom of Alexander, the third
Lord, were, however, eventually recognised. It was
to secure an outlying part of the Earldom in Aberdeen-
shire that Donald had mustered 10,000 men, marched
across Scotland and fought the battle of Harlaw in
1411. The fighting was indecisive, but during the
night the Highlanders retreated. Had they gained a
victory, the history of Scotland might have taken a
different course.

The Treaty of Westminster was revealed to the King
of Scots ; and in 1476 the Lord of the Isles, to make
his peace, was obliged to resign the Earldom of Ross
and Kintyre ; and the title of Lord of the Isles was,
for the first time, conferred upon him by the King.
The proud younger members of the family were furious,
and his nephew, Alexander of Loch Alsh, at the head
of a large force tried to regain the Earldom by arms.

He was defeated ; and in 1493 the Lordship of the Isles was forfeited.

Successive heads of the family had made provision for younger sons by granting them lands to hold under themselves, and large parts of the Lordship and the Earldom were occupied by chiefs of other clans as vassals of the Lord of the Isles. Among them were the two branches of the MacLeods, the MacKinnons, the MacPhees, the MacNeils and the various branches of the MacLeans ; the two latter were particular favourites. To make these provisions proved a severe tax on even the resources of the Lords of the Isles. Some lands were granted successively to different owners, leading to feuds ; and bitter jealousy developed between the cadets of Clan Donald and the most favoured vassals. Nevertheless the kinsfolk of the Lord of the Isles and the island chiefs showed a wonderful fidelity to the Lord of the Isles in his rebellions against the King, and to the claimants who tried to restore the Lordship after it was forfeited.

On the other hand, certain of the mainland vassals, such as the Mackintoshes and the Camerons, sometimes would not follow the Lord of the Isles in opposition to the King, and the chiefs of some clans, such as the MacKays, the Munroes, the Frasers, and, above all, the MacKenzies and the Campbells, were bitterly and consistently opposed to the Lord of the Isles. The two latter laid the foundations of the great positions to which they rose on the ruins of the old Lordship.

There are still vestiges that show the importance of the Lordship as a focus of Gaelic civilisation. The ruins stand of the chain of strong castles that defended the Lord of the Isles' territories, and the site can be

traced of the centre of his power at the great manor of
Finlaggan in Islay. The records of rich donations and
the remains of many little churches, as well as the
greater remains of Keills, Saddell, Oronsay, and Iona,
testify to his piety and that of his people. While
wandering in all parts of his dominions, one can still
note the influence of the old Lordship in the beautiful
standing crosses and tombstones with their interlaced
foliated patterns—a form of art that hardly extended
beyond the confines of the old Lordship and barely
survived its fall.

The family historians tell of the traditional Gaelic
ceremonial at the inauguration of the Lord of the
Isles. In the presence of the clergy, the great men of
the Isles, the poets, and the assembled people, he was
set on a stone marked with a footprint to signify that
he should tread in the steps of his forebears. He was
clad in a white robe to symbolise innocence and
integrity of heart, and that he should be a light to
his people and maintain the true religion. He was
invested with a white rod to symbolise his power to
rule without tyranny or partiality and with discretion
and sincerity, and with his father's sword to signify
his duty to defend his people.

His great domains were administered by a council
of sixteen, made up of representatives of the lords and
the freeholders of the Lordship ; and there was a
judge (*breve*) in every island with a court of appeal in
Islay. The records of the Lordship and the weights
and measures were in charge of special vassals. Traditions have been handed down of the ceremonial at
his great feasts. Some of his charters, framed in the
conventional terms of feudal Scotland, show that he

was surrounded, like a prince, by the officers of state of his household ; but within his dominions he was known by his patronymic of MacDonald, and he granted lands by a traditional Gaelic formula. Centuries later, when the men of his clan were defeated and oppressed after the '45, an English visitor noted that " the poorest and most despicable creature of the name of MacDonald " was prouder than men of property because he bore that name ; and MacDonald was spoken of as *Buachaille nan Eilean*—the Herdsman of the Isles.

Gaelic manuscripts have suffered fearful casualties, such as the wanton destruction of the library at Iona, but those fragments of medieval Scots Gaelic that survive show that the magnificent literature of ancient Erin—the tales of Cuchullin and Deirdre, of Fionn MacCoul and his band of heroes—was still being preserved and even developed. It is more surprising to find Gaelic versions of the ancient legends of Greece. Poets and musicians received recognition and encouragement. The best known of the poets was Muireadach O'Daly, whose descendants, the MacMhuirichs, were the hereditary seanachies to the Lords of the Isles and afterwards to the chiefs of Clanranald. Many traditional tales show that the daily life of the old Gael was shot through with poetry and that the gift of improvising verse was widespread in all ranks. The Book of the Dean of Lismore is a collection of the poetry current in one corner of the Highlands about the end of the fifteenth century. Its quality and variety are amazing.

The Lords of the Isles had their hereditary family of physicians, the MacBeths or Beatons, and several of

their deeply learned treatises survive, with copious
quotations from Latin, Greek, and Arabic authorities.

After the Forfeiture of the Lordship

After the forfeiture of the Lordship, James IV made
several expeditions to the west to enforce the royal
authority over the old vassals of the Lords of the Isles.
He offered the chiefs Crown Charters for the lands
they had held of the Lord of the Isles, and almost
without exception they made their submission and the
King established good relations with them. Then, in
1499, for reasons we do not know, he revoked these
charters, and entrusted Argyll in the south, and
Huntly in the north, with the letting of the lands and
with wide administrative and judicial powers. There
was a serious revolt ; and the king seems to have done
something to reverse his policy. He fell, however, at
Flodden, where many Highlanders fought for him
faithfully.

Unfortunately, for the next hundred years, with a
short interlude of direct rule during James V's man-
hood, the Privy Council continued the disastrous
policy of entrusting Argyll and, to a lesser extent,
Huntly and other lords, with the administration of
the Highlands. The fact that these Lieutenants and
Justiciars were generally interested parties, and that
they tended to gain appreciably after every rising by
the clans whom they were employed to " daunton,"

offered temptations that the leaders of the Campbells in particular accepted with enthusiasm. The lands of the chiefs were held on short leases or by charters that were again and again revoked, and the relations between nearly all the clans were embittered by the irresponsibility of the government in granting the same land to different and rival chiefs. Rival claims to fertile land were at the root of most of the bitter feuds that raged during the sixteenth century. This was the cause of bad relationships between branches of Clan Donald, such, for instance, as that between Clanranald and Sleat, as well as of the feuds between Mackintosh and MacDonald of Keppoch, between Sleat and Mac-Leod of Dunvegan, between the MacDonald chief of Dunyveg and MacLean of Duart, and between Mac-Kenzie of Kintail and Clanranald and Glengarry. The feuds of these larger clans moreover invariably brought in the smaller ones who followed them—as the MacAlisters followed the Lords of Dunyveg, and the Macraes the MacKenzies of Kintail, etc. In the wild history of the Highlands it is not always realised how severe was the economic pressure on the chiefs, on their clansmen and above all on the wretched " broken men " who had lost the land that was their only means of lawful subsistence.

In spite of their bitter feuds, the branches of Clan Donald and their island vassals were willing to combine together, again and again, in supporting, at extreme risk to themselves, the various attempts that were made to revive the Lordship of the Isles. Two were made by Donald Dubh. He was the son of Angus Òg, the legitimatised son of the last Lord. He had been kidnapped as an infant by Atholl, and Argyll had held him prisoner. Argyll, who was his maternal grandfather, declared that he was illegitimate, but all the adherents of the old Lordship regarded him as the lawful Lord of the Isles. He was rescued by " a Fenian exploit " of the men of Glencoe in 1501 and set at the head of almost the entire strength of the old Lordship. After his recapture, Alexander, Lord of Loch Alsh, next to him in the line of succession, made an attempt to seize the Earldom of Ross ; and his son and successor, Sir Donald MacDonald, led a prolonged rising and claimed the Lordship about 1513–17. He alienated his followers by his wild conduct and perished, leaving no male heir ; but Donald Gorm of the House of Sleat, who was now next in succession after the prisoner, Donald Dubh, made an attempt in 1539. He also was well supported, but was mortally wounded when attacking Eilean Donan Castle in Loch Alsh before the rising had got well under way. Finally, in 1545, Donald Dubh once more escaped and led the last and most serious rising. He had a fighting force of 4000 picked men and 160 galleys, and was supported by Henry VIII of England. He died during the rising, and the Lord of Dunyveg, who was at that time the most powerful of the chiefs of branches of Clan Donald, though not in the direct line of succession, was chosen to succeed him ; but he received less general support and the rising collapsed.

With the seventeenth century the general pattern of West Highland history changed. The authority of the king, exercised through the Scots Privy Council, became much stronger. Two of the Clan Donald chiefs, Sleat and Clanranald, were among those specially penalised under the proceedings for the enforcement of the Statutes of Icolmkill. The government was now able to insist on the settlement of the various clan feuds. This, however, was also partly due to the fact that most of the chiefs had gradually been able to obtain a more secure hold on their lands, often through the convenient tenure of the feu. But while the country became more settled, dire economic necessity forced some clans, the MacDonells of Keppoch and the Mac-Donalds of Glencoe among them, to increase their raiding proclivities.

Meanwhile the loyalties of the clans were re-orientated. The old faithfulness, that had brought them out in support of a claimant to the Lordship of the Isles, now rallied them to the cause of the House of Stuart. In the Civil Wars of the seventeenth century and the Jacobite Risings of the eighteenth, the members of Clan Donald showed an unrivalled loyalty.

Two other tendencies that developed in the seventeenth and much more in the eighteenth century must be mentioned. In the first place the esteem for the old Gaelic culture was declining. It lacked any focus, such as the Lordship of the Isles had given. All the centres of learning were Lowland, and the number of Gaelic books printed was extremely few, and limited to small editions of translations of religious works. In Church and State the Gaelic was suspect as Jacobite and Papistical, and its teaching was severely discouraged. The other tendency was the increasing economic strain, as the limited resources of the Highlands proved more and more inadequate to support the rising standard of living of the lairds and the increasing density of the population. The chiefs of one branch of Clan Donald after another, who had

hung on to their lands " be and by the law " for
centuries, were obliged to part with them ; and the
coming of the blackfaced sheep, that were almost the
only source of increased revenue, depopulated the
glens as no foe had ever done.

In the sad story of the emigration of the Highlanders
from their native land, one of the happiest instances
comes from Glengarry. In 1786 a group of the evicted
tenants with their families and sub-tenants, and with
their devoted priest, founded the settlement of Glengarry in Upper Canada. In 1802 this settlement was
increased by a large party of men who had served in a
Fencible Regiment raised by Glengarry ; and to it
also came many less fortunate emigrants from Glengarry, Moidart, and Keppoch. These settlers gave
" a backbone to that part of Canada at the very crisis
in its history." [1] They formed the Glengarry Highlanders, who rendered valiant service in the 1812-14
American attempt to conquer Canada. Meanwhile
their priests had ministered devotedly amongst the
scattered pioneers of the new colony.

The Branches of Clan Donald

These general tendencies affected all the branches
of Clan Donald, but the emphasis varied very greatly.
At the time of the Forfeiture the main branches had
already been formed, as the following list will show :

Branches Founded Before the Lordship.

  1. The MacAlisters, descended from Alasdair, younger
     son of Donald, Lord of Islay, from whom Clan
     Donald takes its name (see p. 27).

[1] C. Fraser Mackintosh, *Antiquarian Notes*, p. 130.

2. The MacIans of Ardnamurchan, descended from Iain Sprangach, younger son of Angus Mór, Lord of Islay, son and successor to Donald aforesaid (see p. 20).

3. The MacDonalds or MacIans of Glencoe, descended from an illegitimate son of Angus Òg, Lord of Islay, the supporter of Robert the Bruce (see p. 22).

Branches Founded During the Lordship.

4. The Clan Ranald of Garmoran, descended from Ranald, son of John, first Lord, and Amy, heiress of the MacRuairidhs (see p. 23). The main cadet branches were Glengarry, descended from Ranald's younger son (see p. 25), Knoydart, and Morar.

5. The Clann MhicIain Mhóir, known as Clan Donald South and the chiefs as the Lords of Dunyveg (from a castle in Islay) and the Glens (from their Irish possessions). Descended from John Mór, second son of John, first Lord of the Isles and Princess Margaret, daughter of Robert II. In the sixteenth century the Irish lands of this branch came into the possession of a younger son and his descendants. The head of that family was in 1644 created Marquess of Antrim. The most important Highland cadet branch was the Clan Ranald Bane of Largie in Kintyre, descended from Ranald, younger son of John Mór (see p. 21).

6. The MacDonalds of Keppoch, less well known as the Clan Ranald of Lochaber. Descended from Alasdair Carach, youngest son of John, first Lord of the Isles, by his second marriage (see p. 26).

7. The MacDonalds of Loch Alsh. Descended from Celestine, son of Alexander, third Lord of the Isles (see p. 20).

8. The MacDonalds of Sleat, also known as Clan Donald
   North, or Clann Uisdein. Descended from Hugh,
   son of Alexander, third Lord of the Isles (see p. 28).

All these branches of Clan Donald had heather
(ling) as their badge. It is well attested as early as
the seventeenth century that heather was the recognised badge of the MacDonalds.

The first branch of Clan Donald to succumb was
the House of Loch Alsh. Most of the lands of the
Lord of Loch Alsh were in Wester Ross, and they
were confirmed to him after his uncle, John, fourth
Lord of the Isles, had resigned the Earldom of Ross.
The Lord of Loch Alsh, however, made a wild attempt
to over-run the earldom, and in consequence the Lordship of the Isles itself was forfeited. Although James
IV treated this family with considerable indulgence,
they headed two more serious risings, and Sir Donald,
the last chief, died while in rebellion in 1527, leaving
no male heir. One of his sisters had married Mac-
Donell of Glengarry, to whom, through this co-heiress,
some of the lands passed.

MacIain of Ardnamurchan had taken a leading part
on the king's side in the troubles with the Lords of
Loch Alsh, one of whom he murdered. He also captured the Lord of Dunyveg with two of his sons, and
handed them over to the authorities, who executed
them. The last Lord of Loch Alsh and the surviving
sons of the Lord of Dunyveg took a terrible revenge
upon MacIain and his sons. Falling out of favour
with the government, the family took to wilder and
wilder courses. A feud developed with MacLean of
Duart, at that time one of the most powerful chiefs in

the Islands. In the course of this feud, MacLean employed Spaniards from the galleon that had taken refuge in Tobermory Bay after the Armada to ravage MacIain's lands. Most disastrous of all, an heiress succeeded, who parted with the superiority of Ardnamurchan to Argyll; and, although her cousins continued to lead the clan, Argyll finally drove them out about 1625. Outlaws and pirates, they eventually found asylum with Lochiel, and took the name of Cameron.

It will be remembered that the MacDonalds of Dunyveg and the Glens were descended from John Mór, younger son of John, first Lord of the Isles. He had been particularly well endowed with lands in the fertile districts of Islay and Kintyre, and by a successful marriage he had also acquired lands (" the Glens ") in Ulster. This Irish connection the family kept up. Donald Balloch, the second chief of this branch, was a noted fighting leader during the reigns of the third and fourth Lords of the Isles. He led expeditions to Inverness, the far north, and Ayrshire, and he was specially associated with John, the fourth Lord, in the Treaty of Westminster with Edward IV. After the Forfeiture of the Lordship, the Lord of Dunyveg had defied the king and the fortunes of the house were reduced to a low ebb. The family then regained the royal favour, and, during most of the sixteenth century, MacDonald of Dunyveg was the most powerful of all the MacDonald chiefs. His valuable lands were indeed too tempting a bait for Argyll and his kinsman, Campbell of Calder. About 1590 the family again lost the royal favour, and Angus, the old chief, and Sir James MacDonald, his son, were enmeshed in a web of intrigue and forced into rebellion. The history of the fall of the house is unusually well documented, and gives a shameful example of the Campbell chiefs' combined activities as *agents provocateurs*, court wire-pullers, judges, executioners, and recipients of the swag. James VI's complicity in the disgraceful affair, in the hope of obtaining augmented rents for Kintyre and Islay, illustrates the fatal disadvantages of the chiefs' position. Islay was lost in 1615, and, with the death of Sir James, the line of Dunyveg became extinct. His kinsman, Colla Ciotach, " Left-handed Coll," known as Colkitto to the Lowlanders, was a redoubtable warrior, but a not over-scrupulous adventurer. His son, Sir Alasdair, joined Montrose with a band of Irish soldiers at the opening of his first campaign, and, as one of his most active lieutenants, played a part in Scots history.

The MacDonalds of Glencoe form one of the most ancient branches, being descended from Angus Òg, the supporter of Bruce. But it was always a small branch, and its members made themselves obnoxious to the authorities by their determined support of the Stuart cause and their activities in cattle lifting. In 1691 all the Highland chiefs had been ordered to take an oath of allegiance to William and Mary under the threat of " the utmost extremity of the law." The authorities had hoped that the more disaffected clans, including several branches of Clan Donald, would refuse, and thus furnish an excuse for their extermination. All, however, took the oath. But MacDonald of Glencoe had put off doing so till the last moment, and stormy weather, and legal quibbles as to whom he should render it, had delayed him till after the

allotted time. By further intrigues the fact that he
had actually taken the oath was then suppressed ; and
Sir John Dalrymple, Under-Secretary of State, took
steps to make an example of him. A party of soldiers
of the Argyll Regiment were sent to Glencoe, and,
thinking that his oath of allegiance had been accepted,
the old chief with his people received them hospitably
and entertained them for ten days. Then, on a bitter
winter's night, the soldiers massacred all on whom they
could lay hands—men, women, and children—in cold
blood. Special parties had been posted, to cut off any
fugitives ; but, with terrible losses, a few survivors
made their way over the hills to Appin. This shocking
deed has earlier parallels hardly less disgraceful in the
treatment of the Highlanders by the Scots Privy Council
and their ministers, although it aroused far greater
public condemnation. The clan, indeed, was not exter-
minated. Its men were "out" in the '15 and the '45, and
the chiefs held their lands until the nineteenth century.

The branch of the Clan Ranald of Garmoran is
descended from Ranald, son of John, first Lord of the Isles
by his first marriage with Amy MacRuairidh. The Lord
of the Isles arranged that he should be succeeded in the
Lordship by Donald, the son of his second marriage
with Margaret, daughter of the Steward, afterwards
Robert II, while Ranald should hold his own mother's
patrimony of the Uists, Garmoran, and other lands
under him. Ranald acquiesced in this arrangement
and acted as tutor (regent) during the minority of
Donald, handing over to him the leadership of the
clan when he came of age. Godfrey, Ranald's full
brother, after his death seized his lands ; and for three
generations he and his descendants styled themselves

Lords of Uist and remained in possession. How Clan-ranald fared is not known. When Godfrey's line died out in 1460, however, they regained their ancestral territory. Unfortunately for them, John, the fourth Lord, then granted some of their lands to his brother, Hugh of Sleat, and there was a renewed struggle. Clanranald, however, contrived to hold their own, and eventually gained full titles to their lands.

Their story furnishes a fine example of the deter-mined support of clansmen to the chief of their choice. An unpopular chief was eliminated—probably killed by his relations. He was succeeded by his uncle, Alexander, to the exclusion of his sons, who were eventually compensated by the grant of territory. Alexander's son, John Mùideartach, succeeded him, and obtained Crown confirmation for his lands. He, however, fell foul of the authorities, and, obeying a royal summons, was imprisoned. A cousin, Ranald Gallda, whose mother was a Fraser of Lovat, was then forced on the clan. He had less right to the chiefship than John Mùideartach as he was the son of Alexander's younger brother. Next, in a sudden change of govern-ment policy in 1540, John Mùideartach was released and Ranald Gallda fled. John Mùideartach well de-served his official description as " a perilous person," and he and his clan in their impregnable hilly country were able to defy the efforts of the Queen Mother, Huntly, Argyll, the Frasers, the Grants, and others to drive him out. His defeat of the Frasers in the bloody battle of Blàr na Léine in 1544 is well known ; and he lived to transmit his lands to his son. Subsequently Clanranald played a most distinguished part in all the efforts for the Stuart cause.

In spite of their stormy history, Clanranald were generous supporters of the old literature of the Gael. They were the patrons of the MacMhuirichs, the hereditary poets of the Lords of the Isles, providing two farms for their maintenance. The MacMhuirichs continued to compose poetry in the traditional Gaelic metres down to the eighteenth century, and they wrote a most valuable history of the MacDonalds.

To the MacDonalds of Benbecula, a cadet branch of Clanranald, belonged two of the most distinguished members of Clan Donald. One was Flora MacDonald, who helped Prince Charles Edward to escape from the Long Island to Skye. The other was Alexander Mac-Donald (Alasdair Mac Mhaighistir Alasdair), perhaps the greatest of modern Highland poets. The son of a clergyman and himself a school teacher, he was well-lettered and a master of both the old and the new metres. His longest work, the " Blessing of the Ship "—the description of a voyage by the galley of Clanranald—has been described as the finest sea-poem written in Britain.

One of the Clanranald chiefs introduced the potato into the Highlands from Ireland in 1743, greatly against the wishes of his clansmen. But his will prevailed and cultivation of the root spread far and wide, to become the people's staff of life. The line of Clanranald weathered the turmoils of the past ; but they fell victims to the economic pressure of more modern times, their lands being sold in the early part of the nineteenth century.

The most important of the branches deriving from Clanranald was that of Glengarry, which is descended from Donald, a younger son of Ranald, the founder.

One of his descendants as chief of Glengarry married a sister of the last Lord of Loch Alsh and inherited lands in Wester Ross ; but unfortunately this brought Glengarry into conflict with the expanding power of MacKenzie of Kintail, to whom these lands were lost. In the sixteenth and early seventeenth century Glengarry had been closely associated with Clanranald ; but the chief achieved great influence during the Commonwealth, when he put up a stout resistance to Cromwell's troops, and also later in Dundee's campaign. So highly was he thought of by Charles II that he was created Lord MacDonell and Aros—he had hoped to be made Earl of Ross in virtue of his descent from the co-heiress of Loch Alsh—and he was treated as the leading chief of Clan Donald. As, however, he left no direct heir and was succeeded by a cousin, the title lapsed. The Glengarry who was contemporary with Sir Walter Scott was a well-known character. He crippled his estate in his fantastic attempts to re-create the ancient state of a Highland chief, and in the nineteenth century the last of the family lands had to be parted with.

The MacDonalds (or MacDonells) of Keppoch were descended from Alasdair Carach, the third son of John, the first Lord. He had valiantly defended the lands of his nephew, Alexander, who had been imprisoned by the king ; and it is therefore surprising that his patrimony in Lochaber was bestowed by the Lord of the Isles upon Mackintosh, who had deserted the Lord of the Isles to join the royal army. The family, however, continued to occupy part of their old territory, sometimes by lease, sometimes by force. In this feud with the Mackintoshes, the last clan battle was fought in 1688 at Mulroy, in which the Mac-Donalds were victorious. They were also bitterly at feud with the Camerons. Loyal Jacobites, one of their best known chiefs rendered formidable service under Dundee—unfortunately he was as formidable to some of his fellow-Jacobites as to their opponents. His nickname of "Coll of the Cows" speaks for itself! He even held Inverness to ransom, and the Burgh was saved only by the intervention of Dundee.

In the fiercest exploits of their struggle for existence the chiefs were loyally supported by their clansmen; and when Keppoch was in exile after the '45, his devoted followers continued to transmit their rents to him. On the other hand, Iain Aluinn, a chief who tried to "appease" Mackintosh by giving up a freebooter to him, was deposed. The family was distinguished by great poetic talent. Some good verse was written by Silis, the daughter of a chief who was himself a poet. But a cousin, known as Iain Lòm, attained real distinction. He was a man of affairs—he was the prime mover in bringing the assassins of his nephew, the young chief, to justice, and it was he who warned Montrose, as he was marching down the Great Glen to attack a Covenanting army in front of him, that Argyll was hastening to overtake him with a yet greater force. Montrose thereupon doubled back through the hills, and defeated Argyll at Inverlochy, while Iain Lòm celebrated his victory in resounding verse. Iain Lòm is notable as one of the first two poets to use the new metres that released the last great flowering of Gaelic poetry. Charles II made him Poet Laureate of Scotland.

The earliest of all off-shoots of Clan Donald, the MacAlisters, remained comparatively small. They occupied lands in Kintyre and their chiefs generally followed their more powerful kinsman, MacDonald of Dunyveg, but they survived long after Argyll had obtained possession of Kintyre. Very early some members of the clan removed to the Lowlands, where they took the name of Alexander ; James VI's favoured minister, whom he made Lord Stirling, was among their descendants.

Finally, and most important of all, there is the branch known as the MacDonalds of Sleat, Clan Donald North, or Clann Uisdein, who are descended from Hugh, son of Alexander, the third Lord. His brother John, fourth Lord, provided him with lands in Skye and also (as mentioned above) with the patrimony of Clanranald. During the early sixteenth century the chiefs had a hard struggle. Black Archibald, one of the wickedest uncles in history, played a murderous part in family quarrels ; their charters were revoked ; and they were at feud with their neighbours —Clanranald and the MacLeods of Dunvegan—for the possession of their lands. By the tenacity of successive chiefs charter rights were regained in 1597. One of the chiefs had even made a bid to recover the Lordship of the Isles. He was supported by most of its old vassals, but at the outset he was mortally wounded and the attempt collapsed. In the seventeenth and eighteenth centuries successive chiefs supported the many struggles of the House of Stuart almost until the last. In 1745, however, when the reigning chief found that Prince Charles Edward had failed to bring the French support for which the Highlanders had stipulated, he refused to imperil his family and his clan in the wild risk of the Rising.

In 1625 Donald Gòrm MacDonald of Sleat had been made a baronet. In 1776 Sir Alexander MacDonald of Sleat received a barony under the style of Lord MacDonald of MacDonald. Since 1947 Lord Mac-Donald has borne the undifferenced arms of the Head of Clan Donald. He still occupies lands of his ancestors, the chiefs of Sleat. Of the state which those chiefs kept, we have a seventeenth-century description by Mary MacLeod. " The lovely country of Duntulm, wherein waxen candles blaze, and wine is drunk right freely there from wan and gleaming cups of silver in a mansion wide and joyous and full of music." [1]

MacDonald of Sleat was one of the last Highland chiefs to maintain a bard. After the family of his old hereditary poets had died out, a distinguished North Uist poet, John MacCodrum, was appointed. His emoluments consisted of a croft rent free, five bolls of meal, five stone of cheese and £2 5s. annually. One of the family seanachies, Hugh MacDonald, wrote a history of the MacDonalds that tells us much of the little we do know about the old Lordship. Sleat was, however, better known as the patron of piping. The MacArthurs, his hereditary pipers, claim formerly to have been pipers to the Lords of the Isles. Piping, however, came into greater esteem in the grimmer days of the sixteenth century. The MacArthurs enjoyed the grant of a farm in virtue of their office, and there they maintained a college of piping. The last of them, " Professor " MacArthur, was piper to the London Highland Society. They were considered to be second only to the MacCrimmons, acknowledged the finest pipers in Scotland.

[1] Tr. by J. Carmichael Watson, *Gaelic Songs of Mary Macleod*, p. 77.

Septs of Clan Donald

Alexander	Mac a'Challies	MacHugh	MacRorie
Allan	MacAllan	MacHutchen	MacRory
Allanson	MacBeth	MacHutcheon	MacRuer
Beath	MacBeath	MacIan	MacRurie
Beaton	MacBheath	Macilreach	MacRury
Bethune	MacBride	Macilriach	MacShannachan
Bowie	MacBurie	Macilleriach	MacSorley
Colson	MacCaishe	Macilrevie	MacSporran
Connall	MacCall	Macilvride	MacSwan
Connell	MacCash	Macilwraith	MacVarish
Currie	MacCeallaich	MacIsaac	MacVurrich
Darroch	MacCodrum	MacKeachan	MacVurie
Donald	MacColl	MacKean	MacWhannell
Donaldson	MacConnell	MacKechnie	Martin
Donillson	MacCook	MacKellachie	May
Donnelson	MacCooish	MacKellaig	Murchie
Drain	MacCrain	MacKelloch	Murchison
Galbraith	MacCuag	MacKeochan	Murdoch
Gilbride	MacCuish	MacKessock	Murdoson
Gorrie	MacCuithein	MacKichan	O'Drain
Gowan	MacCutcheon	MacKillop	O'May
Gowrie	MacDaniell	MacKiggan	O'Shannachan
Hawthorn	Macdrain	MacKinnell	O'Shaig
Henderson	MacEachern	MacKissock	O'Shannaig
Hewison	MacEachin	MacLairish	Philipson
Houstoun	MacEachran	MacLardie	Purcell
Howison	MacElfrish	MacLardy	Revie
Hughson	MacElheran	MacLarty	Reoch
Hutcheonson	MacGeachie	MacLaverty	Riach
Hutcheson	MacGeachin	MacLeverty	Ronald
Hutchinson	MacGillivantic	MacMurchie	Ronaldson
Hutchison	MacGilp	MacMurdo	Rorison
Isles	Macglasrich	MacMurdoch	Sanderson
Johnson	MacGorrie	MacMurrich	Shannon
Kean	MacGorry	MacO'Shannaig	Sorley
Keene	MacGoun	MacPhilip	Sporran
Kellie	MacGowan	MacQuistan	Train
Kelly	MacGown	MacQuisten	Whannel
Kinnell	MacHenry	MacRaith	

Pipe Tunes Associated With Clan Donald

Salutes

Fàilte Chloinn Dhòmhnuìll ..	MacDonald's Salute.
(By Donald Mor MacCrimmon)	
Faicheachd Chloinn Dhòmhnuìll ..	MacDonald of the Isles' Salute, or The Parading of the MacDonalds.
Fàilte an Ridire Séumas nan Eilean..	Sir James MacDonald of the Isles' Salute.
(By W. Macdonald of Vallay)	
Fàilte Baintighearna MhicDhòmhnuill	Lady Margaret MacDonald's Salute.
Fàilte Chloinn Raònuill	Clanranald's Salute.
Blàr na Maòile Ruaidhe	The Battle of Mulroy.
Fàilte Fir Bhaosdail	Boisdale's Salute.
Fàilte Morair Bhàràsdal :. ..	Barrisdale's Salute.
Fàilte Fir Cheannloch Mùideart ..	Kinlochmoidart's Salute.

Gatherings

Làmh Dhearg Chloinn Dhòmhnuill..	The Red Hand of the Macdonalds.
Cruinneachadh Chloinn Raònuill ..	Clanranald's Gathering.
Cnocan Ailein Mhic Iain	Gathering of Clanranald.
Cille Chriosd	Glengarry's March.

Marches

Spaisdearachd Mhic Dhòmhnuill ..	March of the MacDonalds.
Pìòbaireachd Dhòmhnuill Dhuibh ..	Black Donald of the Isles' March.
Spaisdearachd Alasdair Charaich ..	March of Alexander of Keppoch.

Laments

Cumha Morair Chloinn Dhòmhnuill	Lament for Lord MacDonald.
Cumha an Ridire Séumas Mac-Dhòmhnuill nan Eilean	Lament for Sir James Mac-Donald of the Isles.
(By W. Macdonald of Vallay)	
Cumha an Ridire Séumas Mac-Dhòmhnuill nan Eilean	Lament for Sir James Mac-Donald of the Isles.
(By Charles MacArthur)	

Cumha Baintighearna Mhic Dhòmhnuill (By Angus MacArthur, 1790)	Lament for Lady MacDonald.
Cumha Raònuill Mhic Ailein Òig .. (By Donald Mor MacCrimmon)	Lament for Ranald MacDonald of Morar.
Mort Ghlinne Chòmhainn	Massacre of Glencoe.
Cumha Mhic Mhic Alasdair (By A. Monro)	Glengarry's Lament.
Cumha Alasdair Dhéirg	Lament for Alexander MacDonald of Glengarry.
Cumha Dhòmhnuill an Lagain ..	Lament for Donald MacDonald of Glengarry.
Spaisdearachd Dhòmhnuill Ghruamaich	Donald Ghruamach's Lament for his elder brother.
Cumha Taòitir Mhic Dhòmhnuill ..	Lament for MacDonald's Tutor.
Cumha Caisteal Dhun-Naoìmheig ..	Lament for Dunyveg Castle.
Cumha Fir Cheannloch Mùideart ..	Kinlochmoidart's Lament.
Cumha Iarla Antruim	Lament for the Earl of Antrim.

Other Tunes

Cha Clann Dhòmhnuill Socharach ..	The MacDonalds are Simple.
Caismeachd Dhun Truin	The Piper's Warning to his Master.

The Clan Donald Lands Trust

A significant new development illustrates how the Clan has preserved its ancient loyalties, while adjusting them to modern conditions. In 1917 the last of the once vast lands of the Clan Donald had to be sold; but, through the enterprise of a group of devoted clansmen the Clan Donald Lands Trust was formed. Fifteen thousand acres of MacDonald land in Sleat has been saved, and a Clan Donald Centre created at Armadale Castle; the beautiful gardens are being restored and part of the ruined Castle is being converted into a restaurant where visiting clansfolk can meet. There is also a museum, named "The Museum of the Isles." This is a most fitting title, for it commemorates the special service to Gaeldom that the Lordship of the Isles rendered in being the centre for preserving and developing its Arts, its traditions and, above all, a pride in its own identity.